Mrs Joyce Hoover

CW01064414

How Do You D

A Quick'n'Easy Guide to Britain and the British

Mrs Joyce Hoover is a landlady in Brighton, on the south coast of England. She has had more than three decades' experience of cost-conscious catering for overseas visitors, many of whom come to Britain to learn the English language. In recent years she has enjoyed considerable success with her public lectures on British identity, British culture and the importance of learning 'proper English', as used by native speakers such as herself.

Martyn Ford, writer and illustrator, comes from Sutton Coldfield in the West Midlands, while **Peter Legon**, writer and publisher, was brought up in Liverpool and Leeds. They were colleagues at the same Brighton language school where, in 1983, 'Brighton's Leading Landlady' made her very first appearance.

Also published by Lee Gone Publications

The How To Be British Collection

The How To Be British Collection Two

The How To Be British Calendar

Mrs Joyce Hoover's

How Do You Do?

A Quick'n'Easy Guide to Britain and the British

Martyn Ford & Peter Legon

Mrs Joyce Hoover's How Do You Do?
A Quick 'n' Easy Guide To Britain and the British

Published by Lee Gone Publications
11 Kenya Court
Windlesham Gardens
Brighton
East Sussex, BN1 3AU

www.lgpcards.com

First published 2009

©2009 Martyn Ford, Peter Legon

Artwork by Martyn Ford

ISBN 978-0-9522870-5-6

Designed and typeset by folio at Neuadd Bwll, Llanwrtyd Wells
www.foliopublishing.co.uk

Printed by Manor Creative
www.manorcreative.com

1 2 3 4 5 6 7 8 9

For Mrs Turk

BRITAIN!

NORTHERN IRELAND

SCOTLAND

WALES

ENGLAND

DOOR KNOCKER

MY HOUSE is a little United Kingdom. Notice that although the rooms have different names, they are all under the same roof — which is BRITAIN. What is the door? Well, it's how I get in and out of the house, silly!

Contents

Introductions

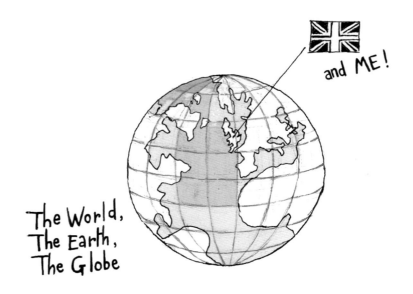

and ME!

The World,
The Earth,
The Globe

Hello. I'm Mrs Hoover. What's your name?

How do you do!

You must answer *How do you do!*

Don't say, 'I do it very well.' And *certainly* don't say, 'Fine, thank you.' Remember, it's not a question, it's an introduction. Look:

ME: *How do you do?*

YOU: *How do you do?*

You see how easy English is?

Well, that's enough about you, let's talk about me.

I'm a landlady. A hostmother. That is to say, I take in foreigners. Oh, dear. I can see you still don't understand. Let me try again: I'm a hostess for foreign visitors to Britain. They stay with me in my home in Brighton as paying guests. It's not expensive and it's better than a hotel or a hostel because THEY EXPERIENCE REAL BRITISH LIFE CLOSE UP AND FIRST HAND.

Sorry, am I shouting? I'm so used to talking to foreigners – Thais, Turks, Taiwanese, Swedes, Swiss and Saudis, Armenians, Americans and Australians – people from all four corners of the globe who are unlucky enough to speak a foreign language. Because of this I have learnt to speak. Slowly. And. Clearly. In. Simple. Words.

My Britain

I t has been statistically proven that, if you are foreign, you are more likely to:

a) live abroad
b) speak a foreign language
c) drive on the wrong side of the road
d) be bitten by a poisonous snake

So it's hardly surprising that the first thing most ambitious, energetic young people around the world want to do when they grow up is to come to Britain.

This book which you have picked up and – I sincerely hope – *paid for*, is about life in Britain.

Perhaps you are thinking, 'Hang on – isn't this just Mrs Hoover's idea of Britain? What about all the other Britains out there?' Well, you're right. This book describes *my* Britain; your Britain (if you have one) may be a bit different from mine. However, as a landlady, who's been trying to explain Britain to overseas visitors for nearly forty years, I think I know more than most about my country, its people and our unique way of life. Although I rarely travel outside East Sussex, my home at 179 Davigdor Road, Hove, near Brighton, is a little United Kingdom. and I'm convinced that wherever you go in these isles, whoever you talk to and whatever the weather, you'll find that what I say in these pages is true – *so true!*

Here and There

When my children were little they used to shout downstairs to me: *Mum! Come here a minute.* And I would always shout back: *No, you come here.*

It's the same today. If any of my former paying guests invite me to visit them in their homes overseas, I always say: *No, you come here.*

You see, Britain is *here* whereas abroad, however much you dress it up, is always *there*. All my life I've always preferred *here* to *there*. It's more convenient, the noises and the smells are more familiar, you can trust the plumbing, you can understand what the people are talking about. And, to be perfectly frank, it's *so much better.*

Where on Earth are We?

Let's start by looking at the geography of Britain.

Our island looks like an old man sitting in the sea off Northern Europe. His head is Scotland (those pieces falling off his face are Scottish islands). He's got a big bottom (East Anglia) and two arms (North and South Wales) and one bony leg (Devon and Cornwall) sticking out into the sea. With this leg Britain is just about to kick Ireland, like a football, far out into the Atlantic Ocean. Some would say, 'And serve it right, too!' But not *me*! Oh no. I love all nationalities and I treat all of them with respect, whether they deserve it or not.

Well, this 'old man of the sea' is Great Britain. It's where we Brits live. All 60 million of us. It looks rather small, doesn't it? Well, size isn't everything and this little island, you should know, is the CENTRE OF WORLD TIME AND SPACE.

How can this be?

Let me explain. In south-east London there is a place called **Greenwich**. (Say *Grenidge*, don't say *Green witch*, or people will point at you and laugh.) At Greenwich there is a famous Observatory and running through this Observatory there is something called the **Prime Meridian Line**. It's the point where east meets west and where each new day and year and millennium start.

The line was discovered in 1773 by a workman called John Harrison when he was replacing some floorboards under the main telescope in the Meridian Building.

The King was informed and immediately map makers, navigators, astronomers and many other clever people rushed to Greenwich to see this wonderful line. At first they were not sure it really *was* the Prime Meridian or not. They stayed at Greenwich arguing about it until 1884, when they finally had to admit that it was correct. They agreed that Greenwich would be 0° longitude and that all journeys in the world would start or end there. They also accepted that Greenwich Mean Time (GMT) was the correct time and set their watches by it. Only France and San Domingo refused to accept it (the French were upset because they had always thought that Paris was the Centre of World Time and Space. Imagine!).

So the next time you check your watch to see if you're early or late for that appointment, and the next time you're sailing around the world and want to know if you are 72° to the west near the coast of Hispaniola, or 68° to the east in the Kazakh Uplands, just spare a thought for John Harrison, the King of England and all the other clever Brits who made it possible to find your way somewhere and get there on time!

How to Get Here and Your Carbon Footprint

When deciding how to travel to Britain nowadays you should think about your **carbon footprint**. This is the sooty deposit you leave behind you when you go on a journey. Too many people these days are moving about the globe without wiping their feet and our poor planet is looking decidedly mucky. Aeroplanes are very bad in this respect and you wouldn't get me up in one. What's more, arriving in Britain by plane is much too quick. You're not prepared for how different it is here and this can cause **culture shock** – the unpleasant feeling of dizziness caused by the sudden realization that another country is better than one's own.

What about entering Britain along the Channel Tunnel?

JET AEROPLANE

WALKING

POGO STICK

Well, you try it if you want – you wouldn't get *me* down there. Knowing all that sea was on top of me would give me the screaming abdabs. How often do they check for cracks in the roof, I'd like to know!

But there are other reasons for staying out of damp dark tunnels under the ocean bed.

The Chunnel was opened in 1994. Before that Britain had been separated from the mainland of Europe for 8,500 years, i.e. since the last Ice Age. During which time we became *Great* Britain. Draw your own conclusions!

In English the word *overseas* is a synonym for *foreign*. Britain is an island, and the sea provides a natural hygienic barrier between us and the rest of the world, one which we bypass at our peril. For this reason, the best way to arrive here is by ship, with a salty wind in your face and the cries of the seagulls in your ears. You can choose between the Atlantic Ocean, the North Sea, the Irish Sea, the Celtic Sea and the English Channel. And as your boat rises and falls over the waves, you can relive the same excitement, curiosity and intense nausea that must have been felt by the Romans, Angles, Danes, Normans and Polish Plumbers who travelled here by the same means all those long years ago.

Our Disappearing Coastline

Being an island means we have a lot of coast. It runs all the way round us – north, south, east, west and many other directions, too. Wherever you are in Britain, if you start walking, whatever the direction, sooner or later you'll reach the sea. Try it. Close your eyes and start walking. You'll know that you're approaching the sea because you'll hear seagulls and you'll feel a salty wind in your face. And you'll know that you've reached the sea when your shoes start to feel wet or when you plunge headlong off one of our many attractive cliffs.

Indeed, one of the most famous (and welcome!) sights in the world is the white line of cliffs you see as you approach the south coast of England by boat across the English Channel. These lovely cliffs are white because they are made of **chalk**. Unfortunately, chalk is a soft, crumbly rock and easily eroded by wind and rain. Bad weather coming in from mainland Europe is gradually causing our chalk cliffs, our coastline in other words, to crumble and fall into the sea. Every year a few more inches of England are lost in this way. Houses, hotels, shops and caravans that were once miles inland find themselves getting closer and closer to the edge. However, it is a long-standing tradition that English folk in this predicament do not turn and run from looming disaster – they stand their ground, literally, until the last crack appears in the chalk and gravity takes over. The south of England has more people living in it than any other part of the country. We need every square inch we can get, because our area is so popular. Yet,

year by year, our region is getting smaller – dissolving like a
sugar lump in a hot cup of tea!

On the Bus

As for getting around Britain once you're here, naturally you'll want to try the traditional ways of seeing the country at its romantic best – from the top of a double decker bus.

Look at what you get for your bus fare:

◆ plush seats (subject to availability)

◆ satellite navigation

◆ high-tech bells that go DING!

◆ state of the art video surveillance of the dodgy passengers on the back seats upstairs

◆ a free newspaper

◆ three buses arriving at the same time (weekdays only)

Keep Left

If you want to explore the country at your own convenience, and you don't care about your impact on the world's climate, then why not hire a car? All the popular tourist destinations, as well as many unpopular ones, are linked by a world-class network of motorways, starting with the M25, which circles around London and is easy to hop on to from Heathrow or Gatwick airports. A favourite day out for many Brits is a stopover on this famous orbital motorway. Families sit in their cars and play I-Spy or count the traffic cones between Junctions 19 and 23. Then the children get out their portable game consoles, salty snacks and brightly coloured drinks, while Mum and Dad listen to the traffic news on FM radio and reminisce about the 'good old days' when the roads were empty and motorists polite; when there were no speed cameras and no Spanish juggernauts on your tail.

Cheap and Cheerful

Britain has so much wonderful cultural heritage to enjoy – castles, museums, art galleries, ruins, monuments, stately homes, all full of fascinating history. But never mind that, let's turn to what most of us are *really* interested in—

Shopping!

Now, hands up if any of you think it's expensive here in the U.K.

Well, you're wrong. This is a **popular misconception**. It's not that Britain is expensive, it's that *your country is too cheap!* But it's true that life here can *seem* expensive to foreigners because we have something called the **strong pound**. It can take a whole shopping trolley full of some foreign currencies just to buy one GB£.

So why is the pound sterling so strong? Well, for one thing because we have looked after it. Other European nations let their currencies go to rack and ruin, acquiring more and more noughts* till in the end it cost half a million of whatever they were just to buy a packet of hair grips.

So a group of these countries got together and decided to all have the same currency, and hope that it would turn out to be a strong one. They called it the **euro**. This was a bad choice of name. The word begins and ends with a vowel, which makes it sound weak – which it is. **Pound**, in contrast, has a strong, no-

---

*   *nought* is the correct word. Don't let me hear you saying zero!

STRONG

WEAK

nonsense consonant at each end, which makes it sound robust, which it is.

And what happened? As soon as they'd got rid of their liras, pesetas, drachmas, schillings, francs, marks, and so on, they realised they'd lost a priceless bit of their national, cultural and historical identity. And in return they'd got something that didn't seem like real money at all, but more like coupons, luncheon vouchers or lottery tickets.

But it was too late to change their minds and have their real currency back again.

The other reason for the **strength** of the British pound is to be found on the notes and coins themselves. If you are lucky enough to have a British banknote on you now, take it out. That's right – you. Go on. Look at it. Who is that woman pictured on the front? As if I needed to ask! Why, it's **Queen Elizabeth II**, of course. Sovereign Monarch and Head of State of the United Kingdom of England, Scotland, Wales and Northern Ireland and all its Dominions and Dependent Territories from Anguilla to the Turks and Caicos, Head of the Commonwealth of Nations,

Commander-in-Chief of the Armed Forces, Lord High Admiral, Supreme Governor of the Church of England (Defender of the Faith), Lord of Mann, and Paramount Chief of Fiji.

What's more she's got a really big crown made of solid gold encrusted with 444 precious stones – *so there!*

Now if you look above Her Majesty's head, under the words 'Bank of England', it says in small letters I PROMISE TO PAY THE BEARER ON DEMAND THE SUM OF ... for example £10. I mean, with someone as important as that on your banknote *you're going to believe it, aren't you?* You'd say to yourself, 'Yes, she'll pay up, for sure. Here's a currency I can trust!' A lot of foreign banknotes have faces on them too but, oh, how different! Either they are shifty-looking presidents with thin moustaches who are here today and gone tomorrow, or they're so-called 'famous' people who you've never actually heard of!

DISCLAIMER

Mrs Hoover wishes to make it clear that whilst her claims regarding the supremacy of the Pound Sterling as a world currency are absolute and incontrovertible, they may not necessarily reflect its actual value in international financial markets in any given period and that consequently neither she nor any members of the Hoover household can be held responsible for any individual or organisation acting upon her claims and thereafter finding themselves with a suitcase full of worthless ten pound notes.

Shoppers' Paradise

Now here's the good news: it's really very economical to shop here, as anyone can see from the huge number of Pound Stores and Charity Shops in every high street. You can get a wonderful range of bargains in high streets all over Britain. On a recent trip to one of the Pound Stores in my own home town of Brighton I bought:

◆ a multi-pack of custard creams

◆ a bunch of washable polyester tulips

◆ a poster of Justin Timberlake

◆ a rubber fish that sings *Take Me To The River* when you press a button (batteries not included)

◆ a bag of bright blue sweets

◆ a Zorro mask

◆ a jumbo tub of scouring powder

◆ six toilet rolls

◆ a bra

ONLY £1 !

TWO FOR THE PRICE OF ONE

and I still got change from a ten-pound note!

What's more, in Britain you don't have to buy new. At one of our many high street Charity Shops (*Help the Feckless, Hedgehogs Protection League,* etc.) you can re-live the fashions of the eighties at knock-down prices, buy a set of coasters of English Country Gardens, find that rare Julio Iglesias LP you've been looking for all these years *and* at the same have the satisfaction of knowing that you're 'doing good'.

And if you are on a *real* economy drive, and determined to spend as little as possible, you can go to one of our many Saturday morning Jumble Sales. These usually take place in primary schools or church halls and if you don't mind 'rummaging' through piles of soiled clothing you can often find, for a few pennies, a decent blouse, underslip or orange polyester cardigan that will be just the thing for doing the garden.

Buy British!

J ust think of all the things that the world owes to Britain: all the products and technologies that enrich our lives. You pour HP brown sauce over your English breakfast, spread Marmite on your toast using a knife made of Sheffield stainless steel; you switch on BBC radio and listen to a song by the Beatles. You stride through the rain, warm and dry in your Burberry

raincoat and Shetland Islands pullover, and you get into your Rolls Royce (your children follow behind on their Raleigh bicycles). You reach into the glove compartment, take out a packet of Smarties and pop a red one into your mouth. Your hand smells nice from the Body Shop moisturiser you rubbed on it this morning.

Now at this point let me address some rumours that have been going around – circulated, no doubt, by mischievous people who want to show these fantastically successful British brands in a bad light. It has been suggested that some of them are not as British as they used to be: that HP sauce, for example, is now manufactured in the Netherlands; or that Smarties are owned by Nestlé and made in Germany; or that Burberry products are assembled in China; or that Rolls Royce is a subsidiary of the German car company BMW; or that the Body Shop was bought up by the French cosmetics giant L'Oréal'

No longer *British*? Is it likely? The very idea!

In any event, what really matters is that in the hearts and minds of people these famous brands are British through and through, and we won't have it any other way!

Because We're Nice

Once you are here, you should make the most of it. Don't be like *some* foreigners here and stay skulking inside your visitor's hole, eating your own food, mingling with your own compatriots, speaking your own language. How much nicer to get *inside* the country, to snuggle up to its people, and to see the world through our shoes.

A word of caution, however. The British today are very diverse in appearance, behaviour and lifestyle, so finding 'typical' Brits to emulate may not be all that straightforward.

Is there any characteristic common to us all that a foreign visitor might be able to observe?

Well, I think there's a lot to be said for the notion of *niceness*. Brits can be more or less any size, shape, colour or religion; they won't necessarily be wearing a Saville Row suit like James Bond, or a tweed skirt like the Queen, but they should be *nice*. To be precise, they should:

- have nice manners
- speak English nicely
- have a nice home
- …in a nice neighbourhood
- …with a nice spouse and children inside
- …and a nice but smelly family pet
- make a nice cup of tea

Nice view of the Sauce Factory (nice work if you can get it)

Nice Curtains

Nice Couple

Nice children

Nice choice of T.V. programme

Nice cup of tea

Nice biscuits

Nice mess

Nice carpet

Nice doggie

Here are some other things to look for which *may* also indicate that you have found a True Brit:

◆ green fingers

◆ hobbies

◆ a teasing sense of humour

◆ a fondness for the 'good old days' when life was simpler

◆ non-conformity

◆ patriotism

◆ mistrust of patriotism

◆ home ownership

◆ level of credit card debt

What Is 'Britain'
(and why should we bother)?

Britain was 'created' so that the Scots and the Welsh wouldn't feel left out when England was top nation, which it was for many generations.* Also the Scots and the Welsh had some picturesque customs and traditions that the English didn't have and felt might brighten up the national CV and prove useful in attracting tourism and foreign investment to these shores. Examples include: unusual costumes, strong drink, sentimental songs, virile sports, piety and beloved poets. Northern Ireland was the bit left over after a long quarrel between the English and the Irish. It didn't have any picturesque traditions, and nobody really wanted it, but the English kindly agreed to govern it for the time being until a proper owner could be found.

These days the idea of Britishness is sadly in decline. Yet we need that common unifying identity more than ever if we're not to end up at one another's throats.

Let's explore what it means to have a nationality.

---

* And still is, of course, but – sshh! – we're not supposed to say that!

National Identity

Of course we must guard against stereotypes: not all Scots are mean, not all Welsh are narrow-minded, not all English are two-faced. On the other hand, there's no smoke without fire, and if everyone says it there must be something in it. I myself accept people as they are, whatever their race, creed, colour, size, shape, age, sexual orientation and… (I nearly said 'class' then, but even I have my limits!). Yes, I accept everyone, as long as they learn our language, adopt our ways, pay on time and don't use all the hot water.

And anyway, when you stop to think about it, what's wrong with stereotypes? I've been one myself for many years. Stereotypes are beacons of identity in a sea of global anonymity.

The present government wants us to have *Identity Cards*. That says it all, doesn't it? They're worried that there are people out there who are walking around thinking *Yes, I live here, but I'm not British, oh dear me no! I'm something else entirely.* The authorities – the Home Secretary and his crew – think that if you have an ID card then you'll know who you are and where you belong and you'll be (to use the fashionable term) a *stakeholder*.

But it's not true!

British people don't need *cards*. And they don't need citizenship exams either. What they need are clear rules and simple examples to follow. At 179 Davigdor Road I play hostess to visitors from all four corners of the globe. In this 'rainbow household' tempers could get frayed and there might be incidents, such as we see in trouble spots around the world, if it weren't for my **Rules of the House**. On their first day in the Hoover house, my new paying guests assemble in the kitchen where they are shown these rules (or 'Commandments' as I prefer to call them) and asked to swear an oath of allegiance in front of Kenneth, my Bull Terrier. Here are a few examples:

◆ *No foreign languages in front of the Hoover family*

◆ *No American English (e.g. 'cookie' instead of 'biscuit')*

◆ *No hanky panky in the bedrooms*

◆ *No alcoholic drinks in the bedrooms (unless you offer me one)*

◆ *No putting your dinner in the dog's dish*

◆ *No take-away foreign food to be smuggled into the house*

◆ *No retuning to the house between 9am and 4.30pm*

◆ *No wearing frilly negligee in front of Mr. Hoover (especially the girls)*

◆ *No criticisms of the British Royal Family, food, weather or TV programmes*

My guests are expected to learn these rules by heart; any infringements are punishable with fines or extra housework, though in practice the rules are very seldom broken. Kenneth sees to that!

International Friendship

It has been said by some ignorant persons around the globe that we British are a coarse, aggressive people prone to fighting and disorder; what's more, that we are particularly hostile towards foreigners. It's not true! The British are an extremely hospitable nation, as you will discover, with a unique tolerance for foreign currency of all denominations. All right, perhaps we *sometimes* give the impression that we are a little bit wary of strangers in our midst. But this is understandable given our troubled island history. Right up until the middle of the eleventh century we endured repeated invasions from hostile foreign powers such as the Romans, the Vikings and the Norman French – not to mention all the Jutes, Picts, Danes, Huns, Goths, Skaters and Chavs in between. An ancestral memory is stirred in us by the sight of foreign features such as red beards and flaxen hair in plaits. An instinctual voice cries out: Invader! Quick! Run to the hills!

But once we get to know them, once we realise that they are not going to burn down our villages and carry off our wives and daughters, we welcome visitors warmly. As long as they are just that – *visitors.* We like our guests to sit on our sofas, sip our tea and admire our soft furnishings, but at a certain point, quite naturally, we want them to *go.* So that we can tidy up and get on with our lives. I mean, no one likes a guest who gets his feet under the table, or starts rummaging through our cupboards or, like Tigger, asking us what's for breakfast!

If too many tourists decided to outstay their welcome, who knows where we'd end up? We should learn from the example of the grey squirrels who came unchecked into this country, took possession of the tree tops and frightened away our timid native red squirrels.

To be on the safe side, let's check that our visitors on arrival are holding a *return* ticket.

Keeping an Eye on You

The other day one of my paying guests (from Estonia, I think) made an interesting observation:

As I'm walking around town I notice what look like cameras on long poles. They are not pointed at the traffic, so I suppose they're not to catch speeding motorists. What are they for?

Let me explain. They *are* cameras as a matter of fact and they are there to give law-abiding citizens (and respectable overseas visitors such as my Estonian girl) peace of mind.

They are placed there, primarily, to monitor the work of local government employees (street sweepers, parking attendants,

and so on) for purposes of staff training and quality control.

But there are many other advantages to these CCTV cameras, as we call them: in the old days, if you dropped a glove in the street you had the devil's own job to get it back, filling in forms at the Police Station, putting advertisements in the local press, sticking up MISSING posters at the railway station. But nowadays it's almost certain to be caught on camera. A member of the surveillance staff at the local control centre will automatically produce a digital *identicon* of you, the owner, circulate it to all the police forces in the country who will then trace you on their vast database, and before you've even registered the loss, an officer will be round to your house in a patrol car restoring the lost glove and giving you a complimentary DNA swab.

It's true some people have objected to these cameras, saying they invade our privacy and infringe our God-given right, as free-born subjects of her Majesty Queen Elizabeth II, to pick our noses in anonymity. Well, my answer to that is a familiar one: if you've got nothing to hide, then you've got nothing to worry about. Unfortunately, in our society today a lot of people *do* have something to hide. Or *someone!*

Let's face it, people will do bad things when they think no one is watching them. Whether it's spitting, dropping litter, shooting passers by or just scowling and kicking an empty drink can along the street, anti-social behaviour is endemic to our cities.

In the old days people endeavoured to be good even when they weren't being watched *because they thought God was watching them.* But now very few people believe in God, so they think they can get away with it. That's why we need another, more credible authority to keep an eye on us 24/7, and who better than the POLICE, or MI5, or if they're tied up, a private security contractor?

And let's look at it in a positive way: we all like having our pictures taken (witness the enormous rise in sales of digital cameras), and in this celebrity-obsessed age we all want to be on TV. We want our share of the limelight, our 'five minutes of fame'. And do you know something else? Most of us try to look our best when we know we're on camera: we straighten up, we flick the hair out of our eyes, we put a spring in our step and we *smile*. A word of warning, however: members of the public are strongly advised *not* to wave at the cameras, pull faces, or in any way draw attention to them as this reduces their effectiveness in crime prevention and makes the staff at the surveillance centres feel self-conscious.

Class Distinctions
(and how to make them)

As we know, when it comes to the behaviour of young people, parental example is all-important. It's my honest opinion that a lot of these problems with binge drinking by eight-year-olds, and decent law-abiding folk being terrorised by so-called 'hoodies' brandishing 'asbos' or 'shooters', is because so few homes these days have a set of napkin rings in the drawer or teacups with matching saucers. This is a question of social class.

Some people say that Britain today is classless, but it's not. It's very important what class you belong to, and your social class can be seen by what you eat and how you eat it; by what you wear and how you wear it; but most of all by what you say and *how you say it*. Millions of people in this country are held back socially, and prevented from fulfilling their human potential, because they speak with strong accents. Take Mrs Baker, for example, at number 181 Davigdor Road. Because her husband drives one of those Japanese people carriers and they go to Gran Canaria for their holidays, she thinks she's just as good as anyone else. But she's not, I'm afraid. As soon as she opens her mouth you can hear the problem: she has a *regional accent*. Like, me she takes foreign students into her home and I can't imagine how the poor dears can understand a word she says, never mind the effect it must have on their English!

I, on the other hand, was lucky enough to have been born

without an accent, which means I can move confidently through all the social spheres and, what's more, I am a suitable model for any overseas student trying to learn proper English.

Forty years ago the class boundaries were much clearer. My family were certainly not well off but my mother had standards. She kept our front step swept and our brass door knocker burnished brightly. She wasn't held back by political correctness from warning us, 'Don't play with the Bakers at number 181 — they are *common*.' We children quickly got the idea: they were lower down the social scale than us and we could be tainted by association. Unfortunately, there's hardly an area of life nowadays that hasn't got coarser and more common, from coloured nylon shirts for cricket players to foul-mouthed TV chefs to celebrities flaunting their affairs/drug binges in the newspapers.

But being common isn't to do with getting drunk/insulting the waiter/swearing/throwing up/showing your knickers *as such* – it's letting it get into the newspapers or doing it without a degree from a good university. To breach good taste and get away with it, you have to have good taste to start with!

Take my word for it, class divisions here are as strong as ever – the difference now is that the lower classes no longer feel ashamed of their manners and appearance. New equal opportunities legislation means they are allowed to appear in so-called reality TV programmes, behave badly and show their ignorance without feeling ashamed.

In the past only the sons and daughters of well-bred, distinguished families were allowed to misbehave in public, but now anyone can. Take James Bond, for example. He may be ruthless, he may be promiscuous, he may destroy a great deal of expensive machinery, but at least he's been to a good school and speaks and dresses nicely. That makes him a good role model for young British men.

Tsk, tsk! wearing trainers with a Savile Row suit!

Social Graces

Julius Caesar, Norman the Conqueror, Napoleon, Adolf Hitler, Saddam Hussein ... over the centuries many foreign tyrants have tried to invade and conquer this island of Great Britain. Tried and failed. Why? Because they weren't polite. They didn't say 'Please'. The British on the other hand have always said Please before they colonized another country and Thank you afterwards. Which is why the sun never set on the British Empire.

So if you're a foreign visitor, you should use these expressions wherever you go

> *Excuse me*
> *Please*
> *Thank you*
> *Sorry*
> *Let me pay for this*

... and you won't go far wrong.

When you ask for something, you can say please at the beginning of the sentence:

Please don't throw me in the sea.

or at the end of the sentence:

Bring me my bow of burning gold/Bring me my arrows of desire, please.

If you do something wrong, say *Sorry* at the beginning of the sentence:

Oh, I'm sorry. I didn't know you were married.
You can also use *Pardon me* instead of *sorry*:
Pardon me. It must be the raw cauliflower I had at lunchtime.

You must also use Sorry when the other person has made the mistake:

Sorry, but those are my trousers you are wearing.

and you can use it when no one has made a mistake:

Sorry, what's the time?

However, there's more to being polite than saying 'please' and 'thank you' all the time, nice though that is. You need to know about British customs and manners. You'll notice that the word 'manners' has an –s on the end. That's because there are lots of them, which apply in different social situations. You just have to learn them by heart and hope you get it right! The advice in the next five sections of my book will help you to do that – but you'll have to pay attention!

First-Name Terms

Too many people you meet nowadays start using your first name right away. This is very rude. It annoys me when some spotty eighteen-year-old in a call centre or at a reception desk says to me: 'Now Joyce, have you filled in form CS 22?' I mean, why do we have titles then, like *Mrs, Mr, Miss* and *Master*? My advice is: keep your distance. A person's first name is like their toilet: you should ask their permission before you use it.

A: Do you mind if I call you Joyce?
B: Yes, dear. It's at the top of the stairs – first door on the right.

Table Manners

Here are some important dos and don'ts for breakfasting, lunching and dining with nice British people. (Well, actually, it's just don'ts, as I'm sure the dos will look after themselves.)

◆ Do not take food from other people's plates, at any rate not with your fingers

◆ Do not stir your tea with your pencil

◆ When you are served pie do not lift the pie crust before eating in order to discover what's inside

◆ Do not wipe your mouth on the other diners (If no napkin is provided you may use your own sleeve but it's important to change sleeves between courses)

◆ Do not belch and then draw attention to yourself by

proclaiming loudly, 'Better out than in!' The occasional inadvertent belch is unavoidable but remember, it's not a competitive sport; still less is it an art form

◆ Do not finish the last drop of gravy on the plate by moving your finger over it like a windscreen wiper

◆ Do not drop your mobile phone into the soup, fish it out with your comb and then proceed to lick it clean. If you *do* drop your phone into the soup call a telecom engineer immediately

◆ Do not intimidate the other diners with your cutlery

Spitting

When I was young it used to be called 'expectorating' and that was a better word for it – just as 'wind' is a more acceptable term than 'f**ting' – and it was very rare, in spite of the fact there was more bronchitis then and paper handkerchiefs hadn't been invented. The only situations where you were allowed to do it were when brushing your teeth or rinsing your mouth out at the dentist's, and even then it had to be done quietly and discreetly. If you had done it in the street, you would have been roundly ticked off by your elders or betters. Sadly, 'ticking off' is now regarded as child abuse, or a violation of human rights, with the result that expectorating is rife amongst the young.

Overseas visitors are strongly urged to avoid this repellent and insanitary practice whilst in Britain. Anyone feeling a need to spit should use a tissue (see 'Hankies', below) or wait until they get back to their own country.

Hankie Panky

It is a fact of life that, all around the world, noses run. It is what you *do* about it that is the mark of a civilised society. In Britain it is not polite to deal with the problem of a dripping nose by noisily sniffing: this will only make people around you more aware of it: they'll tense up waiting for the next sniff and the horrible possibility of it escalating into a real piggy snort. Blowing your nose, on the other hand, is *not* a taboo here, as it is in some other countries, and can be indulged in noisily and lengthily even at public meetings. My father always enjoyed a good explosive sneeze followed by a loud *Paaaaaarrrp!* into a spotted handkerchief, which he would pluck, with a flourish and a shower of loose change, from his waistcoat pocket. The handkerchief or 'hankie' has long been an essential accessory of daily life here, though there are signs that it may be falling out of use amongst the rising generation. If it were true, this would be a sad loss. Think of the many uses of the hankie, apart from the obvious one: dabbing a spot, tying a forget-me-knot, improvising a sun-hat. Where would the violinist be if he didn't have a clean square of Irish linen to drape across his shoulder at the start of the recital? When tears come there's nothing as comforting as a cotton hankie. True, sleeves are a standby, but they make the user look poor, graceless or too humble. And

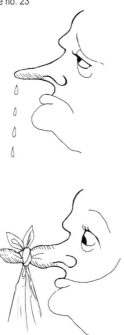

provided that you check first there are no puckered, stuck-together bits, a hankie is also an expressive part of the ritual of saying goodbye. Finally, a lace-trimmed and scented hankie is an indispensable item in a lady's handbag, just as the smartness of a dark gentleman's suit is rounded off by a little peak of silk poking out of the breast pocket.

For more on this fascinating topic, see *A Blow for Freedom: The Hankie in History* by Hoover, J. (Gingham & Crust, 1963)

You-know-what

In my opinion s*x is a subject that is far too openly and frequently discussed in public. Like others of my generation I inherited from my parents a set of long-established inhibitions. And nothing wrong with that. It was through repression, shyness, embarrassment and ignorance about 'you-know-what' that we British were able to build and govern an empire that stretched right round the world *and* make so many Major Contributions to World Civilisation. People say s*x is nothing to be ashamed of. Well, it's nothing to be proud of, either! We all know it goes on, but it should be at a safe distance, out of earshot, and if it is referred to at all should be cloaked with euphemisms, with which the English Language is so well-endowed.

Where 'you-know-what' is concerned, the best advice I can give is keep it under your hat.

A Note On Taboo Words

My guests sometimes ask me, 'What are the rudest words in English? Please tell us, Mrs Hoover, we need to know.' 'But why?' I ask.

'Well, because … ' They look confused and embarrassed.

'So that you can shout them at people in the street?' I suggest.

'No, of course not,' they reply, piously. 'But at least we could understand if British people said them to us.'

Well, readers, I say to you now what I say to my guests: in the unlikely event that a British person used such bad words to you it would be better not to understand them. Indeed, it would be better to stop them right there and say, politely,

'I'm sorry, but I don't understand you. Is there anybody here who speaks English properly?'

Fitting In

Sometimes I'm asked, 'Mrs Hoover, do you think foreigners who come to live in Britain should conform to British customs?'

Now, that's a difficult and very delicate question…

NO – only joking!

It's a perfectly straightforward question.

Of *course* they should, if they know what's good for them! In this age of cultural relativism the idea has got about that one way of doing things is every bit as good as another. It's not true! Imagine if foreigners visiting this country decided to drive their cars on the right hand side because 'that's what we do at home, and our ways are just as good as yours'! Well, the same applies to eating with a knife and fork, being nice to cats and dogs, keeping your front lawn neatly trimmed, wearing your poppy with pride, taking your place in the queue, respecting the Queen, supporting the local Scout Group/Neighbourhood Watch/PCC/Rotary Club/sub-post office, and saying 'please' and 'thank you' at the right time.

Nobody in my corner of East Sussex will ever say, 'Go back to where you came from!' just so long as you respect the local customs.

In some countries it's the custom to take your shoes off when you come into a house, even if you're a guest. This seems strange to me: in my house you might tread in something squishy and mess up your tights, or Kenneth my Bull Terrier might have a go at your feet. However, if I was in such a country I would respect this custom, whatever the hazard to my bunions. (Which is another reason why I avoid travelling abroad.)

The important point to remember is this: Britain is a uniquely tolerant and inclusive society based on liberal values and democratic rights, *and there are very severe penalties for anyone who infringes these!*

Say 'no' to these
(if you want to be British)

◆ Wearing sports clothes when you're not doing sport

◆ Queueing up to write in books of condolence

◆ Making up names for your children. 'Jazmayne' was one I heard recently. What's wrong with plain old 'Janet'?

◆ Talking openly to the media about your problems with alcohol/s*x/wife-beating

◆ Drinking pints of beer at 4 o'clock in the afternoon

- Playing baseball, American football or *boules*

- Supporting Albania in the Eurovision Song Contest

- Having barbecues in your back garden

- Having barbecues in your *front* garden

- Saying things like 'Enjoy your meal', 'Have a nice day', 'You guys'

- Kissing anyone on the cheek, then on the other cheek, and then on the first cheek again!

- Appealing to the European Court of Justice. What's wrong with British laws? They were passed by the 'Mother of all Parliaments'!

What time did you come home last night? Why didn't you phone? You treat this place like a hotel!

THE MOTHER OF ALL PARLIAMENTS

Long to Reign over Us

Unlike most nations divided by differences of class, race, religion and even language, Britain has something special that brings us all together, to which we can all show our allegiance, and that is the Royal Family. They manage to stand for us, represent us and provide us with a model to emulate. They do this by being both ordinary and special.

Politicians have the power to govern (or *think* they have it) but it's the Queen who has the *authority to rule*. If the P.M. is visiting a town people will either not bother to turn up or they will go in order to shout at him, wave placards and, if they get the chance, throw the odd bag of flour. In contrast when the Queen pays a visit communities prepare for months beforehand to give her the warmest possible welcome.

Out come the flowers and the Union Jacks, the mitres and the chains of office, the colourful costumes and the trestle tables with sandwiches and lemonade, the displays of dancing and local crafts, and everywhere the eager faces of young and old lining the pavements, clutching their Union Jacks, hoping against hope for even a glimpse of the only real celebrity on the planet.

In most other nations people are, at best, citizens; we Brits on the other hand are also *subjects* – proud subjects of Her Majesty the Queen, who as we know is above politics (the best position to be).

Nowadays the Queen still opens Parliament and dissolves it, though not just because she feels like it. The monarch no longer leads British Armed Forces into battle, though princes are sometimes detached to the world's trouble spots to keep them out of the tabloid newspapers.

There is a Royal Train and a Royal Jet, but the monarch has had to give up the Royal Yacht (Britannia) and now has to pay taxes, like the rest of us! This is wrong because she is *not* like the rest of us – she's special, and that's why people all around the world admire her and want to be seen with her.

When foreign heads of state come to visit they have to pretend to be interested in meeting and negotiating with the Prime Minister, whereas what they and their wives are *really* looking forward to is meeting the Queen at Buckingham Palace. Wouldn't you be the same? The banqueting hall, the flunkeys, the ceremony, the posh frocks, the protocol, being kept waiting and having to bow or curtsey. Like it was in the good old days!

Most other nations in Europe, indeed the world, got rid of their royal families by cutting their heads off or sending them into exile. Now of course they regret it: they see how beloved our Queen is; how not only Brits but tourists from all four corners of the globe flock to London to visit Buckingham Palace, Windsor Castle and all the other royal landmarks, eager to experience the splendour and the magic of a *real* monarchy! Back home they buy millions of magazines to find out anything they can about the lives and loves of these fairy tale figures. Who, I'd like to know, would amble, let alone 'flock', to France to see the President of the Republic or to Germany to catch a glimpse of the Chancellor??!!

It's true that we English did abolish the monarchy for a short period (1649 – 1660) and even, in a moment of madness, chopped off the king's head. But kings, you know, are rather like worms – chop off the head and they just go and grow another body – and in this case Charles I soon came back as Charles II.

Don't worry, I'll be back!

Delighted To Meet You, Ma'am

If you should be so fortunate as to be addressed in person by a member of the Royal Family, keep your answers short and succinct. Even if you are one of her Majesty's subjects don't assume you are an *interesting* subject. You may well be asked 'And what do you do?' Don't go in to a lot of boring detail on the ins and outs of your job – a short phrase will be quite sufficient. And avoid adding, 'And what about *you*?' In fact, don't ask any questions, least of all ones like, 'Has Edward got a job yet?' or 'What do you really think of Camilla?' A good rule is: Don't speak unless spoken to. Her Majesty has nearly 60 million subjects – she'll never get round them all if you get on your hobby horse! Though talking of which, it is possible you *may* be engaged in conversation about a topic of interest to the royal personage, such as horse racing, polo, dressage, fox hunting, steeplechase, show jumping, equitation and horse breeding, and you should make sure you are well informed on these.

At number 179 Davigdor Road there is a room called the 'back parlour'. Neither my overseas guests nor my husband, Leslie, are allowed to enter this room as it's kept for 'best'. They never see the shining silver candelabra on the highly polished sideboard or the rose-patterned bone china tea set inside. They can only imagine the lace-trimmed tablecloth, the matching table napkins and the set of silver napkin rings to be found in the drawer.

I am sometimes asked, 'Mrs Hoover, what is the point of having a room where no one is allowed to go and a tea set which is never used? What is this "best" for which they are so carefully kept?'

I explain that British ladies, like me, have always dreamt (and sometimes quite literally) that one day they may be honoured by a visit from Her Majesty the Queen. The visit would be unannounced, yet Her Majesty would naturally expect to be served a splendid afternoon tea and not on a stained tablecloth or with chipped cups and plates.

So it is you will always find a fresh Victoria sponge in the cake tin ready to be taken into the back parlour of number 179 just in case the monarch comes calling. After all, such visits date back to King Alfred the Great in the ninth century and it is surely only a matter of time till there's a knock on my door.

LABEL THE PARTS OF
THE HORSE USING THIS
SPECIALIST VOCABULARY

Nose
Tail
Hoof
Mane
Fetlock
Chubb lock
Pastern
Withers
Front end
Back end
Bit you sit on
Accelerator
Brake
Stubborn streak
Minor member of Royal Family

Doing the Honours

In other countries ambitious people want to get to the top; they want money and power so that they can boss other people about.

In Britain it's a bit different: ambitious people want to serve their Queen and their country. They're not interested in making pots of money for themselves. What they *are* interested in, however, is being named in the Honours List. This list, which appears twice a year, includes all those people the Queen decides to honour for being *especially* nice.

The selection is made from a cross-section of modern British society – explorers, business tycoons, actresses, sports personalities, pop stars and chat show hosts. The Prime Minister advises the Queen which ones most deserve an honour. Some of the honours given in this way are:

◆ **The Order of Merit (O.M.)** which is for merit

◆ **The Distinguished Service Order (D.S.O.)** which has extra 'bars' you can add if you're a bit of a collector

◆ **The Order of the British Empire (OBE, CBE, MBE**, etc.) It's obviously a great honour to be associated with the British Empire which once spanned ⅔ of the globe and would still do so today if it hadn't been for certain regrettable historical events

But the best honours to get are those that the Queen decides on by herself. These include:

- **The Most Noble Order of the Garter** which entitles the recipient to wear a colourful piece of elastic at the top of his or her leg with an ancient Latin motto on it. *Honi soit qui mal y pense* (which roughly translates as 'I don't know why you're staring at my thigh'). It's to remind the wearer that he or she shouldn't be proud, because stockings can come down as well as go up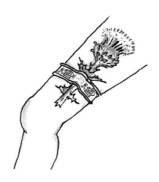

- **The Most Ancient and Most Noble Order of the Thistle.** This is similar to the Order of the Garter but less comfortable (and more ancient)

It's a system that encourages excellence and selfless service to others in the community. Which is why I'm always surprised that no landlady has ever been included in the Honours List. Through our work for the hospitality industry we do so much to represent the British Way of Life in the Best Possible Light to overseas visitors and foreign nationals. Unfortunately some of the advisers our poor monarch has to rely upon are silly prejudiced people who can't see merit when it's staring them in the face!

Religion

O h dear, here's another topic that will have some people shifting uncomfortably in their seats! But we can't ignore religion and it's important that I put you right on it. We Brits pretty much invented religious tolerance, and nowadays we accept all faiths and none, though if pressed I'd say that if you *have to* have a religion, Anglicanism is about the best there is. The Church of England is the Established Church, and it's very definitely a *nice church*. The Queen is in charge of it, helped by a man called the Archbishop of Canterbury. It has been *by Royal Appointment* (i.e. approved by the monarch) ever since Henry VIII kindly set it up in the mid-sixteenth century. Now, I'm not particularly religious myself, but I do go to church as often as I can

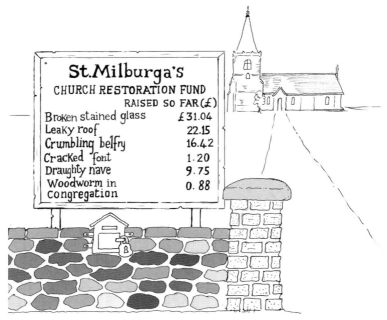

St. Milburga's
CHURCH RESTORATION FUND
RAISED SO FAR (£)
Broken stained glass £31.04
Leaky roof 22.15
Crumbling belfry 16.42
Cracked font 1.20
Draughty nave 9.75
Woodworm in congregation 0.88

a) because it's English and traditional

b) because it's good for you, like five a day

c) so that I can keep an eye on Mrs Baker from number 181 Davigdor Road, and stop her from becoming too powerful on the Parochial Church Council

The good thing is that Anglicans don't worry too much about what you believe or how you worship, or how often, just so long as you're kind to people and can make home-made jam/ring bells/edit newsletters, etc. For most Brits a little religion goes a long way. We are wary of too much *enthusiasm* : we know that the real point of religion is to develop your fund-raising skills, to put your talent for baking or flower arranging to good use, and that a church is a place in which to sit and reflect on those less fortunate than yourself. And of course church makes a lovely and dignified setting for weddings, christenings, funerals and rained-off summer fêtes.

That said, the longer-term visitor may notice that most churches in British towns and cities are now closed or have been turned into discount furniture stores, bars, warehouses, yuppie apartments or lap dancing clubs. This is in line with the new drive to have more community-based worship, or 'outreach' religion.

WARNING: Breast-beating, fasting, processing with lifelike statues, disputing doctrines, proclaiming miracles, wearing 'religious' clothing (unless you're an actual minister) is definitely *not* the way to endear yourself to the right kind of people. And asking others what their beliefs are, or going on about how the Lord said this and the Lord said that, is outright bad manners. In fact, raising the subject of religion at *all* is rather bad form, so I'll stop there!

Beacons of Britishness

s we have seen, the monarch is a **beacon of Britishness** that everyone can recognise. However, **Britain** as an idea has rather fallen out of fashion lately.

To put it bluntly, what would we Brits be willing to die for?

Not, perhaps, our system of spelling or our right to a non-elected upper chamber in the Houses of Parliament.

But what about our right to take our walks in *miles* and buy our cake ingredients in *pounds* and *ounces*?

What about the *Archers*? Or the protection of moths and shrews and wrens? Or our right to eat chips with our Chinese take-away?

To remind us of who we are, we need more Beacons of Britishness like these, aspects of our way of life that people would be willing to lay down their lives for.

(I've even thought of a slogan: Don't Be a *con*, be a *Bea*con – get it?)

Let's examine some of these beacons.

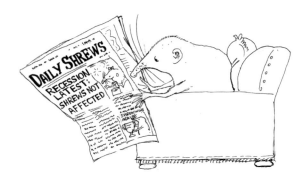

The Bulldog

What could be a better symbol of Britain than this stout-hearted canine: snuffly, rheumy-eyed and bandy-legged, barely able to see through the folds of flesh around its eyes, and capable of only a clumsy waddling run owing to the enormous size of its body relative to its legs. But what courage! Normally placid and loyal, when a Bulldog sees another dog, however big and fierce, it'll 'have a go' at it (especially if it's a foreign breed e.g. Schnauzer, Pomeranian).

Incidentally, **British Bulldog** was for centuries a popular game played by schoolboys. The rules are very complicated and you wouldn't understand even if I explained them but it was a mixture of rugby (without the ball) and freestyle wrestling and the main idea was to lift your opponent off the ground. My brother Roderick played it enthusiastically as a boy and will proudly show you his 'trophies' – a glass eye and a pronounced limp.

Sadly, British Bulldog has gone the way of so many other traditional children's games (Conkers, Marbles, Postman's Knock, Split the Kipper, Squeak Piggy Squeak, etc.) and been banned from playgrounds owing to Health and Safety Regulations.

John Bull

More bull, but this time it's man with a cheery red face (good British beef and beer plus a spot of exertion in the garden), ample stomach squeezed into a waistcoat, side-whiskers and top hat. A bluff, no-nonsense fellow, John Bull loves dogs, owns a few good acres, pays his taxes, goes to church (but hasn't much time for religion) and is proud to tell you that he hasn't opened a book since the day he left school.

Of course, the character of John Bull never existed in reality, which makes him an ideal personification of Britain.

Britannia

We women need our role models, too. There was Boudicca, for example, in the first century AD. She can be called the first Great Briton (at least that anyone has heard of). She repelled the Romans by riding her chariot towards them with one breast exposed. (Which also established our long-lasting reputation for daring and unconventional fashions.) But really the most suitable feminine icon is **Britannia**. She is depicted as a young goddess dressed in white robes sitting on a rock, with a pet lion at her feet. She has a shield and helmet and holds a toasting fork. This is to demonstrate that she is fearless, strong in battle, but nevertheless all woman and able to rustle up afternoon tea at a moment's notice. As with Boudicca her right breast is exposed. This is to show she's not bothered by the cold weather and doesn't care what other people think of her dress sense.

Er... no milk for me, thanks

The Milkman

It's 4.30am and Davigdor Road is dark and silent, except for the faint hum of an electric van labouring along at three miles per hour, and then the squeak of the front gate, the clink of glass bottles on the doorstep and cheery whistle of a departing **milkman**. Like so many Beacons of Britishness, our dear milkman is under threat from the Buy-One-Get-One-Free culture of the supermarket and the 24-hour mini mart. He's survived, but he's had to adapt: pints of 'full cream' and 'semi-skimmed' are not enough, nowadays his little milk float also has to carry fruit juice, eggs, pizza, alcopops, carpets and bootleg DVDs. But the essentials haven't changed, thank goodness: he still has his cheery whistle, and a cheeky wink for us housewives on Saturdays mornings when it's time to pay up! And of course he still forgets that extra gold top we asked for!

The Union Jack

The United Kingdom, like a house that hasn't been properly cared for, seems to be falling apart. But will the separate pieces be worth having, or is the whole more than the sum of its parts? I think we know the answer, don't we? Just consider the individual flags: England's is a red cross on a white background which is not very comforting as it makes you think of accidents and first aid boxes; Scotland's is two diagonal white stripes on a blue background which looks like a sign telling you 'Not Allowed!' or 'Cancelled!' or 'Don't go in there!' etc. All rather negative and off-putting. The Welsh flag is a red dragon on a green and white background and dragons as everyone knows died out long ago. The Northern Ireland flag is the red cross of St George with a white star in the middle and a rather puzzling red glove on it. Whose glove is it? Where is the other one? And is there a matching hat and scarf somewhere?

But if you put these flags together in the Union Jack you have a very different and much more attractive design: the white diagonals of Scotland are embellished with nice red stripes and the blue is broken into lots of interesting triangles and there's the cross of St George in the middle still to show how England is at the centre holding it all together. The Welsh flag is not included though because the green would obviously clash with the blue (and there isn't room anyway). All in all this combination of verticals, horizontals and diagonals makes a nice harmonious pattern that is ideally suited to mugs, towels, teapots, teddy bears and underpants.

Lords and Commons

Our Parliament consists of two chambers: the House of Commons, where the Members we elect debate the urgent political issues of the day, and the House of Lords, which is a kind of day centre for politicians who have become too elderly and frail to tolerate the noisy proceedings of the Commons. The House of Lords is also known as the Upper House, because the members are usually of a higher social class than those in the Commons (who are more common). Peers that have time to attend can discuss, in a calmer atmosphere, things that are more important to ordinary British people, such as Daylight Saving and the protection of garden birds. Both chambers are **steeped in tradition**, but the House of Lords is more deeply steeped and so I prefer it. There are more ceremonies, and the wigs, robes and other regalia are of better quality.

Miles Better

Britain has gone a long way in introducing metric weights and measures. Children in our schools are taught about kilometres and kilograms; they draw triangles in centimetres, and record temperatures in celsius. You can buy a litre of cooking oil at the supermarket and order square metres of carpet for your sitting room.

But it's not us. We are only going through the motions. We do it out of courtesy to our near neighbours in continental Europe, who can only calculate in tens and feel uncomfortable if numbers don't have a nought on the end (a memory of their defunct currencies, perhaps?).

The true Brit thinks in dozens and grosses, remembers fondly when there were twelve pennies to a shilling and two and a half shillings made half a crown and twenty-one shillings

were a guinea. In the days when the measure of the world was *imperial* you could still ask for a stone of potatoes, and a field was measured in chains and furlongs. Even today, patriotic Britons insist on buying their curtain material in yards and their tobacco by the ounce. It's true that our American cousins have also held on to their miles and their gallons but, frankly, they're not as good as their British originals. For example, a British gallon is equal to 4.5 litres, whereas for an American gallon you only get 3.785 litres!

Not that you'd *want* litres anyway, of course. I mean, if your friend said to you: *Do you fancy going out for 0.568 of a litre of beer tonight?* what would you think? Would you want to go? Would you want to see that person ever again?

We've already lost the quart, the bushel and the scruple; the hundredweight and the acre are clearly in danger. But the Euro modernisers are not going to stop there: they want to metricate every inch (*inch,* note) of our lives.

Recently a few selfless Brits have paid a high price defending our cherished system of weights and measures. These so-called 'Metric Martyrs' have gone to gaol for our right to eat apples by the pound, do thirty-five miles to the gallon and stand six foot tall in our stockinged feet

Let's hope their sacrifice will not have been in vain!

They didn't know it yet, but the
Grammar Police were everywhere...

English, Please!

Millions of foreigners all around the world use English to communicate with each other. This is now so common that it has led to the error of supposing that the English of these *non-native speakers*, as they are called, is just as good as ours. It is important to remember that our language is called *English* because it comes from *England*, and was created and nurtured by the genius of the English people, especially those of us who live in my particular corner of East Sussex.

We don't mind other nationalities borrowing our language, providing they acknowledge where they got it from and refer any disputes over grammar and usage to *us*.

Here is an example of a typical conversation between two non-native speakers using English as the medium of communication:

FOREIGNER 1: *Do you go this night in the cinema?*

FOREIGNER 2: *Yes, it is.*

FOREIGNER 1: *That is well. We can to meet us in the near from it.*

FOREIGNER 2: *I go there. At what o'clock?*

FOREIGNER 1: *At 15 after 8, before the cinema.*

FOREIGNER 2: *Yes, it is.*

A brave attempt, maybe, but it hardly compares with the noble language spoken by William Shakespeare, Winston Churchill, Margaret Thatcher, or Sir David (and Lady) Beckham.

But it's not just a question of elegance; correct and

unambiguous English can be a matter of life and death. All over the world people are working with dangerous machinery, toxic chemicals or precision surgical instruments, and they're talking about it *in English*. One mispronounced syllable, one false preposition, one irregular verb awry and disaster can follow.

BALLISTICS OFFICER 1: *Since it's Christmas shall we detonate the nuclear warhead?*
BALLISTICS OFFICER 2: *All right. I'll press the button.*
BALLISTICS OFFICER 1: *Sorry, I meant decorate it.*
BALLISTICS OFFICER 2: *Pardon? Ah, there it goes! Cover your eyes!*

My Mother's Tongue

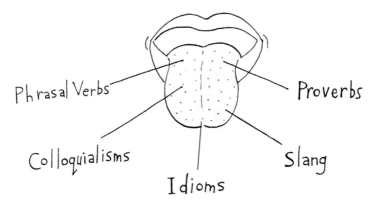

The diagram above shows the importance of learning your English from a **native speaker** like myself. English is my mother tongue, the language I inherited from my mother and which she inherited from her mother. There were more 'choice expressions' on my mother's tongue than you'd find in a whole library of English Language text books!

English is the language of world politics, the language of international trade and finance, the language of computers and information technology, the language of science and medicine, the language of pop music, films and fashion and the language of international travel and tourism. Ornithologists tell us that parrots, mynah birds, canaries, etc. prefer speaking English to any other language. And the few individuals who have made contact with aliens from other galaxies all confirm that *the language they used to communicate with them was English!*

He says, Do we speak Moldovan?

You can see why so few British people learn to speak foreign languages – it just isn't necessary!

Perhaps one day other languages will die out and everyone in the world will learn English as their mother tongue. But until that happy day the important priority for most people who want to get on in life is to come to England, study English by rubbing up against the people who spoke it first and still speak it best, i.e. us English! (Or is it 'we English'? Don't ask me, I'm not a grammarian!)

English is the richest and most complex language in the world, with the longest history, and yet it is the easiest of all languages to learn. Why is this?

Well, for one thing, it doesn't have all those silly case endings for masculine, feminine, singular, plural, accusative, dative, locative, genital, etc. that most other languages have (I mean, who cares whether a toothbrush is male or female?). What's more it only has one word for YOU instead of two or three, so when you have to speak to someone you don't have to stop in order to work out their age or status or your exact degree of intimacy with them.

On the other hand, English has a very wide vocabulary. For example, in most languages you can say, 'It's raining' or 'It isn't raining', and that's about all. Or perhaps you can say, 'It's raining a lot' and 'It's raining a little'. But that's as far as you can go. In English, on the other hand, there's a whole wealth of expressions for this important area of human experience, from 'I think I felt a spot of rain' to 'Here we go again!' Here is a handy list of them for you to learn by heart so that you can use them confidently whenever you meet a British person in the street and want to strike up a conversation.

Joyce's Weather Words

- It's just a bit of drizzle
- It's only a shower
- It's pouring
- It's teeming
- It's pelting down
- It's bucketing down
- It's raining cats and dogs
- It's absolutely chucking it down
- It's coming down in stair rods

"... I tink I feel a spot of rain just now...."

However, in this era of climate change it's important that your conversational repertoire should reflect what's really happening in the world. Britain no longer has the distinction of being the dampest, cloudiest place on earth, and you should be prepared to chat about *extreme* weather conditions, as these will occur more and more frequently:

A: *Turned out wet today, hasn't it?*

B: *Yes, it has, hasn't it? But we should be all right clinging to this tree.*

A: *Excuse me. I wonder if you could spare a drop of water?*

B: *Sorry. I'd love to, but I need it to irrigate my guavas.*

On the plus side, the hotter temperatures mean that in Sussex, where I live, there are now vineyards, which means that I can drink wine without being unpatriotic. Malaria and sandstorms seem a small price to pay for such a pleasure!

A Good Laugh

O ne important thing you should know is that you'll never get on well with British people if you can't take a joke.

It's natural for us to tease and make fun of each other. Nothing is sacred here and being foreign or a visitor is no excuse!

Legs are there to be pulled, so get used to it!

The most important priority for speakers of other languages is understanding jokes in the first place.

Q: *Why is it useless to ask a newspaper reporter what he puts on his dinner?*

A: *Because a good journalist never reveals his sauces.*

Now, did you laugh at that joke?

You didn't?

Well, that's almost certainly because you speak a foreign language and you just didn't 'get it'.

Sauces are what you put on your dinner (at least *we* do) and *sources* are where a journalist gets his information from. The two words sound the same. This is an example of a **pun**.

Now do you get it?

Look, try these puns:

◆ *Time flies like an arrow; fruit flies like a banana.*

- *He drove his expensive car into a tree and found out how the Mercedes bends.*

- *Police were called to a children's nursery where a three-year-old was resisting a rest.*

- *If you don't pay your exorcist you get repossessed.*

- *To some marriage is a word; to others it's a sentence.*

- *I used to be a tap dancer – until I fell in the sink.*

Well?

Oh, come on, you're not trying! If you were a native speaker you'd be in stitches by now!

The point is this: if you're going to be here amongst us for some time, you should make an effort to understand our puns. First, because it's polite to laugh when someone tells you a joke (they'll think you are miserable or unfriendly if you don't), and second because everywhere you go in Britain there are puns all around you. For example, there's a hairdressing salon near me called *Curl Up and Dye*.

Get it?

The thing is, puns are enjoyable. You can have fun with a pun!

Here is one of my all-time favourites:

1ST COURTIER: *The Queen seems very grumpy this afternoon.*
2ND COURTIER: *Don't worry, she'll be fine when the strolling players arrive.*
1ST COURTIER: *Oh, so it's just pre-minstrel tension?*

But even if you *don't* understand such jokes, I strongly advise you to laugh at them. People will think you're very clever and, more to the point, very well-integrated into British life. And if you can actually make your *own* original puns during a conversation people will be very impressed indeed and may even begin to treat you as an equal.

For goodness' sake don't say: 'These British jokes aren't funny!' Believe me, they *are* – it's just that you can't see it yet. But live here long enough and you will.

The Cup that Cheers

The favourite drink of the British, as everyone knows, is tea. Everyone, that is, except the British themselves, who seem to have forgotten it. There was a time when a 'cuppa' was the response to almost any turn of events, be it good:

—*Mother, guess what. I've just been made President of the World Bank.*
—*Well done, dear. I'll go and put the kettle on.*

or bad:

—*Doris. I'm afraid I've lost the house and all our furniture in a poker game.*
—*That's a shame, dear. I'll go and put the kettle on.*
—*But Doris, it's worse than that: I bet you as well … and lost!*
—*Oh, well, never mind. Let's have a nice bit of fruit cake with it, too.*

Now, sadly, young and not-so-young Brits flock to the corporate coffee bars that have taken over our town centres to drink *cappuccinos, skinny lattes, macchiatos, mochas, double shot espressos, Americanos.* It's come to something when you have to have A-level Italian just to order a hot drink!

Of course a lot of un-British fashions like this have come here from the United States. Think what the Americans did in 1773: they boarded a ship in Boston Harbour, took the cargo of English tea and threw it into the sea. What a silly thing to do

What To Drink

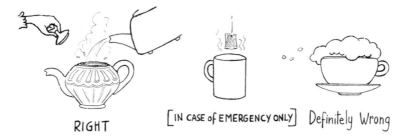

RIGHT

[IN CASE of EMERGENCY ONLY]   Definitely Wrong

Keep It Hot

Heat Inside

HEAT LOST ↑

RIGHT

WRONG

Diagram showing the importance of the cosy to a Satisfying Tea Experience

How To Drink (nicely)

WRONG

Pinkie [@45° extension]

PINKIE EXTENDER (available from all good pharmacists)

Nourishing Accompaniments

doily

Famous 'London transport-style' double-decker teatime plate for cakes and biscuits showing traditional doily.

– everyone knows that you need *hot* water to make tea! From that day on the Americans decided that coffee should be their national beverage instead. And to show their determination, they fought a War of Independence against the British. And we all know the problems *that* led to!

Tea is obviously a superior drink to coffee. Tea revives, refreshes, restores, relaxes, rejuvenates … and lots of other things beginning with *re-*. What's more it's much better for you than coffee, as we can see from these diagrams from a medical text book (*see figs. 1 &2*).

It's my belief that in such a situation as this, drinking tea, brewed in a pot, and poured into proper teacups with saucers, is not just a pleasure, it's a patriotic duty.

We should be more like the Japanese, who have held on to their traditions: in Japan, tea is served by pretty girls in traditional costume who spend years learning how to boil a kettle, how to put the teabag into the pot with a graceful movement, how to pour the tea out without spilling any in the saucer and how to hand round the biscuits to the guests before helping themselves.

We older Brits should, as a matter of the highest priority, teach the younger generation our own distinctive teatime traditions before it is too late.

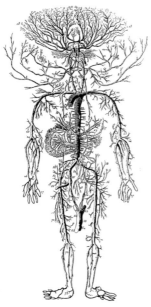

Fig 1 Here you see the nervous system of a typical Italian after a strong cup of espresso coffee. Look at the nerves all jarred and jangly. No wonder Italians are always shouting and waving their arms about!

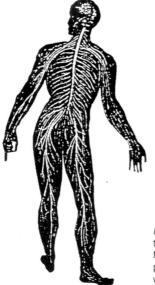

Fig 2 Here, by contrast, is the nervous system of a typical British person after two or three cups of tea. Notice the nerves calmy arranged in symmetrical patterns and the posture relaxed and natural. No wonder Brits are known for keeping a cool in a crisis!

Greater Britons

The good news for you Brit-lovers is that there's a lot more of us nowadays. And I'm not talking about numbers of people. No, it's a statistical fact that the average Brit today is 3½ stone heavier than the average Brit fifty years ago.

Some people disapprove of this. They say it's not healthy; that we are snack-guzzling, binge-drinking couch potatoes. This is not fair: I won't hear our national vegetable slandered in such a way.

In reality you and I know lots of ladies, size 20 or above, who are perfectly happy, well-rounded personalities. They may not look good in lycra shorts but they can cook well, smile nicely, sing and give you a nice warm hug when you need it. And it's not so important if you can't tie your shoelaces, because many styles of shoes these days come with Velcro fasteners, and young people who wear trainers don't bother to tie the laces even if they *can* reach them.

But what are the reasons for this expansion of the population?

Well, there are more shops selling more food than ever before. We certainly didn't have all these huge supermarkets when I was a child. Mrs Partlett's little shop at the corner of our street sold flour, sugar, butter, tinned peas, custard powder, clothes pegs and one variety of detergent. And that was all. Anything more exotic and you had to undertake a long and arduous journey into the city centre and take your chances in one of the smarter grocer's shops. Nowadays my local *Costco* stocks twenty-three varieties of chocolate biscuit and fifty-six varieties of pasta alone!

Greater Britons!

This diagram shows how Britons have gone on developing over the last 120 years.

1890   **1950**   **2010**

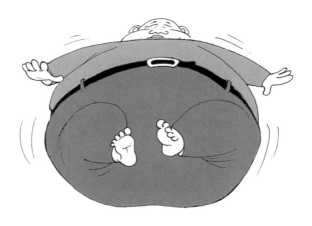

2070 (projected figure)

Other people say that it's because our diet these days is higher in fat and sugar. This is not true. I grew up during a period of 'classic' English cooking where most foods were fried in lard and the snack of choice was a hunk of bread with beef dripping sprinkled with salt. Perhaps we didn't have Death by Chocolate or Banoffee Pie, but we did have suet puddings and jam roly poly. And when we sat down in the evening to listen to the radio we thought nothing of eating a whole tin of treacle and a couple of tins of condensed milk between us. There was none of this namby-pamby, semi-skimmed, lo-carb, reduced fat, caffeine-free nonsense. What's more, everyone had five or six spoons of white sugar in their tea.

It's true that we all had false teeth by the time we were thirty, but we were as skinny as greyhounds. That's because we were always physically active. I walked eighteen miles to school and back every day. When the weather was bad I used to have to start out the day before in order to arrive on time in the morning. What's more, we had no labour-saving devices at home so we all had to roll up our sleeves and help my mother with the sweeping, scrubbing, scouring, dusting, polishing, washing and ironing, and after that help our father with the digging, mowing, building, plumbing, painting and car maintenance.

All this incessant physical activity kept us thin. And of course smoking sixty untipped cigarettes a day probably helped (back in the good old days when it didn't harm your health). I'm as thin as I've always been, and that's because I'm always on the go, rushing around looking after the needs of my international household of paying guests. Which is why I still have the ankles of a woman half my age.

The Food of Greatness

Britain has one of the greatest cuisines in the world. It's a mystery to me why it's not known outside Britain. I haven't space here to describe the huge variety of national and regional dishes that have nourished Great Britons since time immemorial. However, let me list a few 'must tries' which you must try.

Fish and Chips

Fish   Chips

Everyone, even envious and resentful foreigners, must have heard of our celebrated fish and chips. It's true that the British were not the first people in the world to think of catching fish with nets or lines, and then cooking and eating them, but it was the British who had the brilliant idea of coating the fish in flour, egg and milk and dropping it into a vat of boiling black oil, and then (a peculiar stroke of genius, this) using the same oil to deep fry sticks of potato with which to fill up the rest of the plate.

The Pie

But there's more to British food than battered cod and fried potato.

As well as parliamentary democracy, flushing toilets and the world-wide web, Britain has given the world a wonderful wealth of PIES.

Celebration Fish Pie
Steak and Kidney Pie
Potato Pie
Melton Mowbray Pork Pie
Apple and Blackberry Pie
Mince Pies
Banoffee Pie
Humble Pie
Four and Twenty Blackbird Pie

In English if we want to heap praise on something we find really excellent we say that it's *'as nice as pie'*.

There's a pie for every day of the year. Basically a pie is any sloppy mixture containing lumps of something, with a **pastry** lid over it.

Ah, but you need to know the secret of how to make perfect pastry that sticks to the roof of your mouth. And I'm certainly not going to give away our national secrets!

Baked Beans

East West, Home's Best, – not least because it's the only place where you can find those little reddish-orange beans in a nice sweet but zesty 'tomato' sauce that are so loved by every true-born Brit. No full English breakfast is complete without them and they make a filling lunchtime snack on a couple of rounds of toast. In many countries beans are all different shapes and colours, and as hard as stones. They have to be soaked in water overnight to remove all the toxins and boiled for several hours to soften them. And after that they need lots of tummy-upsetting herbs and spices just to make them edible! British baked beans by contrast can be enjoyed by anyone at a moment's notice. No skill is required: just open the tin and tip the contents into a saucepan.

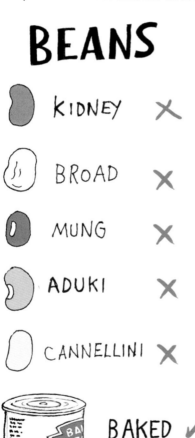

Yet another example of British hi-tech solutions to age-old problems!

Gravy

When the continentals talk about **sauces** they usually mean hot liquids with vegetable stock in them and herbs and probably a dollop of wine too. For us Brits sauces are cold and come in bottles. And they're either red (tomato **ketchup**) or brown (**brown sauce**). If you're going to pour a hot liquid on to an *English* dinner please make sure it's **gravy**.

This is a wonderful concoction made of the fat and juices which have dripped from the meat while it was roasting. Mix these with a little flour, lots of stock and a generous splash of **gravy browning**, decant into a **gravy boat** and then engulf your sliced beef and puffed up Yorkshire pudding with the steaming hot liquid!

Gravy is something uniquely British. It's so highly prized that we even have an idiom, *to be on the gravy train*, which means to be in a specially privileged position with lots of benefits that other people don't have (i.e. to be British).

Gravy

Custard

Custard

Bright sunshine yellow. Smooth. Sweet. Hot.

'What is it made of, this wondrous English cream?'

'Why have I never heard of this before?'

The kind of questions my guests blurt out when they see their first jug of custard.

But don't ask questions, just pour it on your puddings. Apple crumble. Jam roly-poly. Spotted dick. You'll never want to go home again.

(But you must.)

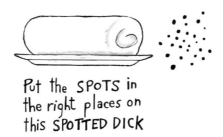

Put the SPOTS in the right places on this SPOTTED DICK

Breakfast

The rule with breakfast is: don't eat anything that sounds foreign. Which leaves out difficult-to-pronounce foods such as *croissant*, *muesli* and *pains au chocolat*. I always serve my paying guests honest Anglo-Saxon fare like porridge, bacon, egg, beans, toast, and CocaCrunchieMegaPops. Oh, and while we're on the subject, there's also an important distinction between **jam** and **marmalade**. It's like this. The fruit…oh, come on… I'm doing all the work here. Why don't you find out for yourself? Ask any Brit – they'll tell you!

Potatoes

Every cuisine has its **starchy staple**, I mean the cheaper stuff on your dinner plate that fills you up. Bulk food. *Carbohydrates,* to use the technical word. In some countries it's pasta, in others it might be rice or noodles. Well, let me state it loud and clear so that none of you out there can say you didn't know: TRUE BRITISH FOLK EAT POTATOES.

Potatoes are created by Mother Nature. They grow in the soil (and sometimes at the bottom of your shopping basket if you forget to take them out). British potatoes are fed by British rain, nourished by British sun, fertilised by British manure. They link us to the land we love and on which we depend. With their portly round shapes, their thick bumpy skins and their tasteless white flesh, they remind us of ourselves. Where, by contrast, does *pasta* come from? Where on earth does it grow? Nobody knows!

Our love affair with the potato started when the Elizabethan explorer and adventurer **Sir Walter Raleigh** brought a couple of pounds back from the New World at the end of the sixteenth

Alas, poor Raleigh! I knew him, Horatio...

century. Up until then Britons had been living exclusively on turnips, and they couldn't believe their luck. At once the native genius of our cooks got to work and before long every weekly household menu included boiled, roast, chips, mash, jacket and spicy wedges with the beef and carrots. So proud are we of our adopted national vegetable that we've even given it royal status by naming our favourite variety the *King Edward.*

Crisps or Chips?

Don't mix up **chips** and **crisps**. Chips are the world-renowned accompaniment to battered fried fish. They should be large, limp, oily and so hot that when you pop one in your mouth you go 'Oo-oh-hohh-hohh-ohh!' and flap your hand in front of your face. Crisps (which were also invented by the British) are factory-made thin slices of fried potato, salty, crunchy and available in different flavours such as cheese 'n' onion, salt 'n' vinegar or grapefruit 'n' anchovy. They are sold (cold, of course) in sealed bags, and are popular with children as an alternative to meals. There *are* also, I regret to say, things called 'tortilla chips', a confusing import from the Spanish-speaking world. I'd like to make it clear I disapprove of this hijacking of the word 'chips' to describe something that is in effect a rather dusty, starchy *crisp.* It's only because we Brits neglected to copyright the word *chip* that the tortilla merchants have got away with it.

The Sandwich

Did you know that it was an English gentleman who invented the famous bread-wrapped snack whose popularity has since spread all over the world? The original (and in my opinion, greatest) example of 'fast food' was the creation of John Montague, the 11th Earl of Sandwich. He had the bright idea of putting his dinner between two slices of bread so that he wouldn't have to interrupt the marathon card games that were his main occupation. Those early sandwiches must have been pretty messy affairs, though, since they involved chops, vegetables, gravy and so on – Nutella and Marmite not having been invented yet!

Encouraged by the international success of his eating innovation, the Earl sponsored Captain James Cook to go and discover the Sandwich Islands (now Hawaii).

So, readers, there's an issue of national pride involved when it comes to choosing between a sandwich and a *baguette* at your local lunch counter!

Cheddar Cheese

Is what you should put *in* your sandwiches. Nowadays you can buy Canadian cheddar, Irish cheddar, New Zealand cheddar, and for all I know Ukrainian cheddar. But you shouldn't! Never forget that real cheddar comes from Cheddar, of course, which is in Somerset in England. If you descend the famous **gorge** by rope right to the bottom, in the dripping darkness of the limestone caves you can sample the world-famous cheese in its original setting.

Cheddar Cheese – the very name, with its pleasing steam-train chuff of alliteration, welcomes you to a whole world of cheesy pleasure. Slice it, dice it, grate it, eat it – you'll be eating a little piece of England.

As the years go by, and your tongue hardens and your taste buds shrivel, you'll go from strength to strength – literally. Mild to medium to mature to extra mature until at last you arrive at Cheese Heaven: Special Extra Reserve *Vintage* Cheddar. It's sharp enough to shave a hedgehog. Believe me, you won't want to go back to those gooey, sweaty-foot-smelling continental cheeses!

NOTE: Apparently, Cheddar Man is Britain's oldest complete skeleton, proof that doubling your intake of our favourite cheese will have lasting health benefits.

Healthy Eating

The British government's healthy eating campaign has been urging us all to eat five portions of fruit or vegetables every day. This is nothing new to me, of course: I've always given my international guests at least five processed peas with their fish fingers and a lot more than five tinned pineapple chunks for pudding afterwards.

But let's be honest, it's a lot of hard work preparing and cooking fresh vegetables every day of the week: swede and cabbage, for example, both require hours and hours of boiling, and all that steam can't be good for the environment. I would love to eat more fruit but it's very acidic and brings on my diverticulitis. However, in case I suddenly feel the urgent need for something fruity and natural I always carry a packet of fruit gums in my handbag. And when you think about it, eating an orange is hard work, isn't it? You have to peel it, remove the pith, cut the skin off each segment, and then, when you've eaten it, have a thorough wash and spend five minutes picking the stringy bits from between your teeth. It's an awful lot easier (and, let's face it, much nicer) to open a tin of mandarin segments, pop them in a glass dish and serve with evaporated milk.

Now it's obviously very kind of the government to worry so much about our health and nutrition. But is it enough? I mean, why stop at *five* a day? And why limit it to time-consuming vegetables and hard-to-digest fruit? I have come up with my own **EIGHT-a-day regime**, consisting of the sort of well-balanced, traditional snack foods that have kept me a 'lean mean catering machine' for all these years. Yes, we need cabbage and potatoes, and we need them every day, but remember our bodies *need* sugar and fat too: sugar to give us energy to solve all the pressing problems in the world, and fat to lubricate our joints, especially as we get older. *Fig. 1* shows the healthy knee joint of someone with plenty of fat in their diet. *Fig. 2* illustrates the danger of 'rusty joint' syndrome caused by recklessly cutting out cream cakes, cheese on toast, pork pie, etc.

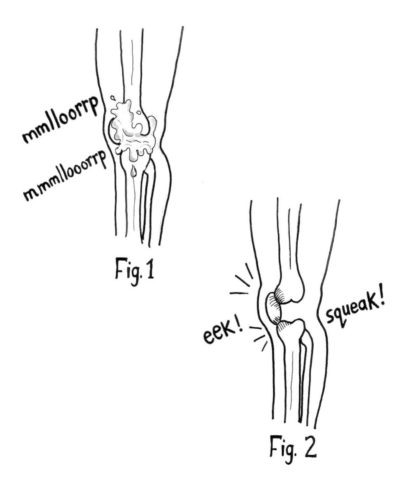

Fig. 1

Fig. 2

My '8-a-day' healthy eating regime

a slice of Swiss roll for elevenses

a fresh cream eclair at lunchtime

a few 'jammie dodgers' at tea time

two or three fairy cakes, also at tea time

a couple of jam tarts 'as and when'

a '99' when out for a stroll along Brighton's famous promenade

a handful of pork scratchings with a glass of sherry in the evening

a few teaspoonfuls of honey/lemon curd/ treacle on a slice of bread, as prescribed by the doctor

My Little Weakness

A song by Mrs Joyce Hoover

The experts tell us cakes are wrong
And those who eat them won't live long
A cake-free diet we should try
But I for one would rather die
Why—?

Because I like biscuits, I like cake
And all the patisseries patissiers make
I've had a sweet tooth since I was eight
And now I have a sweet dental plate.

Jaffa cakes and custard creams
I even eat them in my dreams
I feed my husband and my lodgers
On battenburg and jammie dodgers.

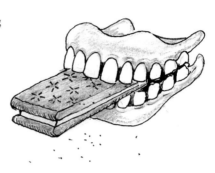

CHORUS
I like biscuits, I like cake… etc.

The doctor says I've put on weight
From all the sugary things I ate
The Church condemns it as a vice
But I don't care, 'cos cake is NICE!

CHORUS
I like biscuits, I like cake… etc.

Someone we should not forget
Is good Queen Marie Antoinette
She told those peasants: 'Eat some cake!
And cheer up, for goodness' sake!'

CHORUS
She liked biscuits, she liked cake
And all the patisseries patissiers make
Those boring peasants wanted bread
And so Queen Marie lost her head!

Well, whatever turns you on
But treacle tart and a sticky bun,
Victoria sponge, with royal icing
And raspberry jam – well, that is MY
thing.

CHORUS
I like biscuits, I like cake… etc.

To have your cake and eat it too
Is quite a difficult thing to do
To have some cake and then to chew it
Is easier – why don't we do it!?

CHORUS
I like biscuits, I like cake… etc.

To feed the world and save the planet –
It can't be all that difficult, can it?
I dream that all men shall be free
At 4 o'clock for scones and tea!

CHORUS
I like biscuits, I like cake… etc.

Homing Instinct

'Home is where the heart is'; 'East, West, Home's Best'; 'an Englishman's home is his castle'. The English Language is full of sayings which show how important the idea of home is to the true Brit. 'There's no place like home'; 'we've put grandpa in a home' … there are so many of them!

Did you know that we call the counties around London (Essex, Kent, Surrey, Middlesex) the **Home Counties**? And that our beloved BBC Radio 4 used to go by the name The BBC **Home Service**. What's more the government department which in other countries would be called the Ministry of Internal Affairs (conjuring up a sinister image of faceless bureaucrats and possibly underground interrogation rooms) in Britain is known by the positively *cosy* title the **Home Office**. And the friendly hospitable man or woman in charge of it is the **Home Secretary**.

But unlike folk on the mainland of Europe the great majority of Brits never really feel **at home** in a rented flat. Everyone wants to get on the property ladder. This is not a real ladder, but a metaphor for buying your first house. However, if you are on this ladder but carrying a heavy mortgage, your foot can slip and you can fall off. The injury this causes will be real not metaphorical.

The ideal British home is a traditional semi-detached house built between 1935 and 1959. It is made of red brick and has a gravel drive, a front garden with a laburnum tree and a back garden with a bird bath perhaps or a gnome fishing peacefully by an artificial pond, a red-tiled roof for the rain to run down

with a chimney on top with a little plume of grey smoke coming out from the **real fire** inside. Most foreign homes, it's well known, have cold marble floors with the occasional small rug, if you're lucky. British homes have wall-to-wall carpets with lively **floral patterns**. When you drop breakables in a foreign home they shatter into a thousand pieces; when you drop your cup of tea/glass of sherry in a British home, it bounces safely up and down on the carpet. Foreign homes have blinds or shutters on the windows, which make the rooms dark and gloomy; British homes on the other hand have fabric curtains in nice bright **floral patterns**, with **nets** for extra privacy.

The aim of these furnishings and fittings is to make a home cosy. Cosy is an important word in every Brit's vocabulary. It's why we wear fluffy slippers and have teddy bear shaped hot water bottles in bed – because they make us feel cosy. It's the reason I still use my fireplace for a nice coal fire – because it makes the room more **cosy** (or, as we say in Sussex, **cosier**). We Brits even have an object which we call a cosy. It's a knitted woollen covering designed to keep things warm – that teddy bear-shaped hot water bottle, for example. Or a fresh pot of tea. Or a recently boiled egg. British ladies knit these cosies by hand, employing ancient skills handed down from generation to generation, and they give them as presents. It is a great honour to receive one.

The Pub

'Pub' is short for 'public house', and a proper British pub should have all the warmth and familiarity of a private *house* (see above) with the noisy fun and sense of danger of a *public* place. The homeliness is supplied by the fireplace and the tables, chairs, curtains, carpets, pictures and ornaments that are scattered around (especially at 'chucking out time'); also by the landlord and landlady who serve and chat to customers and try to keep an 'orderly house'. The thrill of the unknown is provided by the 'public' who turn up there. Those who go there regularly are known as the 'regulars'. The pub is their 'local', which means that they are local people living locally in the locality.

One thing most foreign visitors never remember is the name of the pub they were in the evening before. This is nothing to do with how much they drank there (most of them in my experience sit nursing the same glass of warm coca cola the whole evening) – it's a question of cultural knowledge. As every Brit knows, it matters a great deal whether you were in the Black Lion or the White Swan, the Queen's Head or the Fox and Hounds. Such names are full of history and folklore – if you can be bothered to look them up.

Pubs in town centres these days are places for HVVD – High Volume Vertical Drinking. This tradition started many years ago when pubs were only open for a few hours each evening and naturally customers had a short time in which to get 'tanked up'. Nowadays the licensing laws have been relaxed and many pubs will serve drinks until 2am or until the last customer is carried out

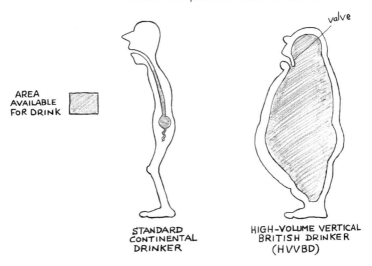

Diagram showing relative capacities
of British compared to other drinkers

valve

AREA
AVAILABLE
FoR DRINK

STANDARD
CONTINENTAL
DRINKER

HIGH-VOLUME VERTICAL
BRITISH DRINKER
(HVVBD)

by staff and the serious private drinking (called a 'lock in') starts. However these extended hours have not made much difference because HVVD is an established part of the British Way of Life and therefore a custom to be cherished and defended.

HEALTH & SAFETY NOTE:

Foreigners should not attempt to copy this style of drinking. The British have got used to it over many generations (see diagram). It can have disastrous consequences for more delicate foreign constitutions.

The visitor should get used to buying his or her 'round' of drinks. The British do not take kindly to spongers – i.e. people, as the saying goes, 'with short arms and deep pockets'. And don't think just because a British friend has asked you to come to the pub with him that he has 'invited' you in the continental sense of 'agreeing to foot the whole bill'. This may work in Europe where most people only ever have one drink (and that frequently a soft one!) but in Britain, where a night at the pub normally involves nine or ten trips to the bar, it can be financially crippling.

When you are at the pub with a group of friends, don't refuse a drink as it may give offence.

Wherever possible you should stick to British drinks. In practice this means mostly 'real ale' (from local breweries), Scottish whisky or 'Scotch', London gin and West Country cider. You can also try some of our classic English wines – apricot, elderberry, damson, parsnip, cauliflower, etc., which many good pubs have on draught. And nowadays – don't gasp – thanks to global warming there are new varieties of British wines (well, let's be honest, *English* wines) that are actually made from English grapes!

In many of the smaller pubs you can still enjoy traditional games (and I don't mean on a giant television screen!). These are tests of skill, strength or endurance that have diverted British drinkers for hundreds of years: table skittles, darts, dominoes, shove ha'penny, cribbage, prize fighting, and pickled onion throwing. In spite of these attractions, surprisingly many British pubs are finding it hard to maintain customer levels. By the way, I'm sure such worries would be a thing of the past if they tried out a game that I regularly play with my students at 179 Davigdor Road – Pass the Pea. This exciting battle of wits involves teams of players passing a pea from one tongue to another (no hands allowed!). When it reaches the end of the line that player has to spin round three times – without dropping the pea, of course – then run to the other end of the line, reciting the phrase

The pea's in play
Prepare the way!

which always sounds more like

Thuh fees in fay
Thefare thuh ray

and then begin the circuit again. Each successful circuit is called a 'pod', and the winning team is the one that makes the most 'pods' before the pea falls off or is accidentally swallowed.

Hours of hilarious fun guaranteed!

Nothing prepares foreign visitors for the raw excitement of traditional games like Pass the Pea.

In large towns and cities nowadays the saloon bar of the typical pub spills out into the street or square and young people are encouraged by the local chambers of commerce to make use of these depopulated public areas of the city for exercise and recreation (traditionally called 'larking about') and as improvised toilet facilities.

Some British Events to be Proud of

There are many special days in Britain. In fact, when you're British every day is special, and when you go abroad (which I try to avoid) people notice that you are special, have special needs and so on, and they respect you for it. Tuesday is always a special day for me because that's when the Hove Hanging Basket and Loose Cover Society have their weekly meeting. I am this year's Chairwoman for Life. However, I'm not going to write about *that* day – you can read the minutes if you want to (I've got them all, going back to 1972).

Instead, here are some of the special occasions in the year that make me proud to be British. They bind us together like garden twine binding a rangy hydrangea.

Foreigners are welcome to come to these occasions as long as they stand at a respectful distance, learn what they mean and how they are celebrated, and refrain from making snide comments about 'antiquated customs'.

Wimbledon

Don't forget that we British invented or at least codified the rules for most sports and games, for example, football, rugby, hockey, horse racing, golf, cricket and lawn tennis, of course, which was probably invented by Henry VIII as a way of meeting girls.

Wimbledon Essentials

Silly patriotic hat

Umbrella (to be left on train)

Sleeping bag (for long queues)

Pimms

Strawberry   Cream

Carrier bag against showers (empty before use)

Fan Banner

COME ON !

insert name of latest British hopeful

The greatest tennis tournament in the world takes place at Wimbledon in London every June and it's a must for every loyal Brit or student of Britishness. Tickets are in great demand (most of them are bought up months before by celebrities who want to raise their profile by being spotted in the crowd watching centre court, where all the top tennis stars or 'seeds' appear). Prepare to queue for several days to get a standing room only one-day ticket for court number 17 or a tuft of grass on Murray Mountain (formerly Henman Hill) outside the grounds.

The matches are played on grass – as it should be. This grass or 'lawn' is so valuable that the players are fined if they damage it by hitting the ball too hard or running about too much. If it starts to rain the Head Groundsman is summoned. He looks at the sky then shakes his head solemnly as a signal for the covers to be quickly pulled over the precious court. The players retire to their dressing rooms to play ping-pong and give interviews to the media. (Putting a roof over a tennis court is *not* what it's all about.)

However the real fun of Wimbledon is not sitting through boring tennis matches for hours on end, exposed to the sun and rain, but wandering round and enjoying the atmosphere of the club at this exciting time of the year: the strawberries and cream, the jugs of *Pimms*, the banners, the funny hats, the (English-style) Mexican waves led by younger members of the Royal Family.

If you are a football fan you have to follow your team's progress over nine months of the year, which can be expensive as well as nerve-racking. The good thing about tennis is you can ignore it entirely for fifty weeks of the year, and then, for the 'Wimbledon fortnight', work yourself up into a state of high excitement, rushing to the radio or TV at every free moment to catch up on the day's play – or at least until the last British player has been knocked out of the championship (usually Day Three of the first week) at which point you are allowed to turn over to Celebrity Beach Volleyball on Channel 91.

The Last Night of the Proms

A night when Brits can display their patriotic pride without embarrassment. The Proms are a series of 'Promenade Concerts' which are not held (as the name suggests) on the seafront at Brighton or Blackpool but at the Albert Hall in London. The 'promenaders' pay homage to the greats of British music by cheering, tooting, waving flags and letting off party poppers through some of their most famous works. Sir Edward Elgar, Gustav Holst (although he had a foreign name), Ralph Von Williams, Benjamin Britten, Sir Edward Elgar, and er, the other one, you know, who wrote the Arrival of the Queen of wherever it was, what was his name? Very famous. You know. Hook or

Strap or something like that. Handel! That was it. Though he was German, wasn't he … ? Anyway, don't be put off by the fact that it's all classical music – a lot of the pieces are almost easy listening and you're encouraged to sing along and join in the conducting, toilet roll throwing, etc.

The nations not so blest as thee
Must, in their turn, to tyrants fall,
While thou shalt flourish great and free:
The dread and envy of them all.

Chorus:
Rule, Britannia! Britannia, rule the waves!
Britons never, never, never shall be slaves.

Words as true and relevant now as the day they were written!

The Chelsea Flower Show

Brits have the greenest fingers on the globe, so naturally Britain is home to the greatest horticultural show of them all. Marvel at our manifold native varieties of chrysanthemum and double dahlia, pansy and petunia. Here you can see what the country's top gardeners can achieve, but remember all of us can enjoy this most British of hobbies, whatever our social standing, whatever our resources. Whether it's an acre and a half with a greenhouse and a croquet lawn, a windswept allotment on the edge of a council estate, a paved patio behind a city terrace, a roof garden on a block of flats, or just a humble window box, we can all experience the same struggle to tame

I'll probably buy myself a bigger pot but apart from that, no, I don't think it'll make a lot of difference...

the elemental forces of Nature that have marked the evolution of Man from hunter-gatherer into TV celebrity gardener. I knew a woman who lived in a dingy one-room basement flat in Brighton who even managed to take a pride in cultivating some rare mildews in her kitchen cupboard!

The Boat Race

An exciting rowing contest between students at Oxford and Cambridge Universities to show that the best of our young people are not only very clever but strong and vigorous as well! The race starts at Putney on the River Thames and is 4 miles 374 yards long (Imperial measurements). It's been going on since 1829. In 1836 it took the rowers 36 minutes to finish; in 2007 it took them less than 18 minutes. This proves that Brits are twice

as fast (i.e. strong) as they used to be. In 500 years from now they should have it down to less than 5 minutes, though it will then be invisible to the naked eye.

The spectators who line the banks of the river to watch are hoping for a bit of excitement and controversy e.g. the clashing of oars, boat bumping, overtaking on the inside, sinking your opponent, etc. Of course, being British, we're very sporting about it and always cheer on the boat that's fallen behind. So far Cambridge has won it a few times more than Oxford. But the patriotic thrill of it is this: whatever the result, the race will always be won by the best university in the whole world!

Crufts

The greatest dog show on earth. For four days in March you can go along to the National Exhibition Centre in Birmingham and cheer on classic British breeds like the King Charles Spaniel and the Bull Terrier as they and their owners are put through their paces. It's not just a beauty contest – dogs have to perform in tests of skill such as Fetch the Slipper, Scratch the Door, Bite the Postman, Sniff out the Asylum Seeker, as well as displays of synchronised barking.

Crufts is a fine example of an 'inclusive' multi-racial society

CRUFTS COMPETITIVE EVENT
Nº 72 : SNIFFING THE GUEST'S PRIVATES

at work: just because you're a foreign breed like a Schnauzer or a Shih-Tzu doesn't mean you can't compete with the great British breeds and even win the coveted prizes of Best Bitch in Show and Ugliest Owner. Though I draw the line at some of these novelty cross-breeds like the 'labradoodle' and the 'peekaboo' which have appeared lately and are definitely not what Nature intended!

The London to Brighton Veteran Car Rally

In my home city of Brighton and Hove we love a good rally, whether it's Minis, motorbikes, bicycles or hostess trolleys. The

most famous of these is the Veteran and Vintage car run which takes place annually on the first Sunday in November. Some of the old crocks taking part are over 100 years old. Their vehicles are pretty ancient, too! They dress up in period clothing, driving goggles, with blankets over their legs, and drive their beloved 'Genevieve' (or roll or push it) all the way from London to the seafront at Brighton. Townsfolk and visitors line the route to wave at the surviving drivers. It's a charming recreation of the golden age of motoring: fifteen miles an hour on thin wheels with spokes, with plenty of bangs and pops and gouts of steam along the way. Is it dangerous? Well, in those sorts of vehicles at that time of the year you are more likely to die of exposure than by crashing into something.

Every year that I watch the rally come in, and wave at those plucky old motorists, their eyes weeping from the fumes and the cold, I reflect with satisfaction, but no real surprise, 'People will do anything to come here!'

Eternally British

Time and time again I get letters like this from disappointed visitors:

Dear Joyce

Oh dear! Britain is so different from what we expected! Where are the friendly London bobbies stopping to tell us the time? Where are the Lords and Ladies strolling up and down Pall Mall? Where is the fog? Where is Swinging London? Everyone we meet wears middle-class clothes but has lower-class manners. The only polite people in the queue for fish and chips are the ones with foreign accents, like us! Could it be that those Life in Britain books that we read so avidly with our English teachers, back in our own country, were wrong?

The culture shock experienced by that correspondent is, I'm afraid, typical. The painful truth is that Britain has changed, and is still changing; it's no longer *the land that time forgot.* Only a few years ago it was still 1955 in most parts of Britain, but now, all of a sudden, the 21st century has arrived here, too. The good news, however, is that we don't *have to* accept it if we don't want to. There may be a few little things we can adopt and benefit from (such as energy-saving light bulbs) but the rest we can safely ignore. Most of it will be a nine-days' wonder anyway. It's not just the old *songs* that are the best — most old things (and I speak as one myself) are nicer than most new things. And if you don't think so now, you will when you're old!

You see, readers, national identity, which gets everyone so worked up these days, is just a matter of continuity, which means doing what your forbears did. Why do so many people assume that society has to *change*? We don't want to put modern concrete roof tiles on a thatched cottage, do we? Or stone cladding on a half-timbered Tudor house. So why should I change? Landladies like me are as much a part of Britain's heritage as the Changing of the Guard or the Edinburgh Tattoo. Citizens unsure whether they are British or English or Lancastrian or Pakistani or (Heaven forbid) *European*, look to us to set an example. How should a British person talk? How should they walk? What should they eat? What songs should they sing? Where should they go on Bank Holidays?

Here's a final question: do people come to Britain to eat tapas, drink cappuccino, ride around in rickshaws, watch American football and have barbecues in the back garden? Or do they come here to eat fish and chips, drink tea, watch cricket, hear the chimes of Big Ben from a red double-decker bus, and dance around a maypole with bells on their ankles?

I think we all know the answer, don't we?

The great thing about us British is our glorious Past, which is just as present now as it was in the past (when it was, of course, the present). Here, the old-fashioned is always in fashion. As I say to the young people I meet — 'Look to your seniors! Get out of touch! The youth revolution's over now. *Old* is the new *new*!'

Postscript

Well, that's the end of my little book about Britain. I hope you have enjoyed reading it. I suggest you read it again now in case you missed something. It was a lot of trouble to write, so I do hope you haven't *skipped* any bits. I get very cross if I cook a nice English dinner for my paying guests and then one of them leaves half of it piled up on the side of the plate. 'You won't get any pudding, if you don't eat up,' I tell them. And I mean it.

If you would like to share with me your own experiences of living in Britain (or, indeed, your own ideas about being British) then you can write to me:

Mrs Joyce Hoover
c/o **LGP**
11 Kenya Court
Windlesham Gardens
East Sussex
GB BN1 3AU

Or if you are one of those young people who don't know how to hold a fountain pen, and don't have a pad of writing paper and envelopes in your desk drawer, then you can type a message instead, using the Internet. The address is

joyce@mrshoover.com

Bye-bye. Come again soon.

This is your book (I hope!) so why not personalise it with your own details?

Your Name:

Signature:

Date:

Your nationality:

Favourite British tradition:

Favourite pie:

Favourite landlady:

Your weight before arriving in the UK:

Your weight now:

Mrs Hoover can be booked for theatre shows or conference events. Contact martyn@mrshoover.com

THIS PAGE MAY BE PHOTOCOPIED